PRESENCE: OVERWHELMED BY GOD
J.D. Greear

Small-Group Experience written by
Spence Shelton

Presence: Overwhelmed by God
Small-Group Study Guide
Published by LifeWay Press®
©2011 J.D. Greear

ISBN 978-1-4158-6987-1
Item 005371605

Dewey Decimal Classification: 231.7
Subject Headings: GOD \ MOSES \ SPIRITUAL LIFE

All Scripture quotations are taken from the Holman Christian Standard Bible®, copyright © 1999, 2000, 2002, 2003 by Holman Bible Publishers. Used by permission.

To order additional copies of this resource, order online at *www.lifeway.com*; write LifeWay Small Groups; One LifeWay Plaza; Nashville, TN 37234-0175; fax order to (615) 251-5933; or call toll-free (800) 458-2772.

Printed in the United States of America

Leadership and Adult Publishing
LifeWay Church Resources
One LifeWay Plaza
Nashville, TN 37234-0175

CONTENTS

BEHIND THE CURTAIN

Over the years I've noticed that there are two kinds of Christians in our church. One kind loves to learn doctrines about God. They treat church like a classroom and take copious notes while I preach. The other loves experience. They love *feeling* the presence of God.

True Christianity is both. It is not just knowledge, nor is it just feeling. True Christianity is a felt experience that grows out of God's revelation of Himself, His character, and what He's done to save us.

The Book of Exodus is the story of God establishing His presence among His people. God reveals Himself to His people in a way that they are swept up in His glory and His love. You can be, too.

"Presence" is the point of Christianity. When you're in pain, what you need are not just doctrines about how God is working it all for good (as important as they are); what you need is the touch of a Savior who has been through pain Himself and walks with you through yours. Our God is a God who knows what it is to lose a child, to be betrayed by a friend, and to be alienated from a Father.

Maybe your Christianity feels a little dry. At times mine sure does. I pray that this study of God's revelation of Himself in Exodus will overwhelm your heart with His love for you. True intimacy with God is grounded in what God has done to save us.

This study was one of the most meaningful our church has ever done. I pray it is a blessing to you as well.

J.D. Greear

ABOUT THIS STUDY

Welcome to *Presence: Overwhelmed by God*—a small-group Bible study from the *Platform* series. In this small-group experience, best-selling author and pastor J.D. Greear takes illustrations from Moses' interaction with the Lord to help us examine the yearning of our own hearts and determine if what we long for is God's blessing or His presence.

Here are the elements you'll be encountering during this small-group experience:

- **Warm-Up** – a time for sharing stories
- **Video Set Up** – establishes context for your small-group time
- **Viewer Guide** – integral points from the video message to enhance discussion
- **Biblical Background** – biblical insight for greater understanding
- **Scripture** – all primary Scriptures are printed in the study guide
- **Small-Group Questions** – application, self-revelation, interpretation, or observation (discovery Bible study method builds community, invites God in, and generates transformational discussion)
- **Journal** – contributes to personal devotional time
- **You're Up** – a challenge for group members to practice what they have learned
- **Leader Notes** - in colored text at the beginning of each section

Presence of God

What is the point of life? Why are we here? Questions about the purpose of life are considered the ultimate questions of human existence and have captivated the deepest of thinkers for thousands of years. During the next six weeks, we will look at the story of the Exodus and how Moses came to understand the presence of God to be life's greatest attainment. We will see that what must define our reality is the simple yet profound truth that God is here, and God is ours.

It has been said that blessings from God are like the warmth that comes from the rays of the sun. Though we can feel the warmth of the rays, we know they are not the source of the heat. The rays direct us back to the sun. In the same way, the blessings of God should direct our hearts back to their Source. We must not substitute the gifts of God for God Himself.

In this session we are confronted with a simple but piercing concept. Do we desire the blessing of God more than the presence of God?

WARM UP

Try not to spend too much time here, but let everyone answer the warm-up questions. Getting group members involved early helps create the best small-group environment. If this is the first time the group is meeting, make sure everyone works on learning names.

List the top three things you can't imagine living without (phone, computer, chocolate, etc.).

What makes these things so critical to your daily life?

VIDEO SET UP

The information below sets up the video. It can be read aloud to the group, read by group members ahead of time, or group members can read the information silently while the facilitator sets up the video.

Most religious systems are built around how we are supposed to interact with God. Commands to follow, ethical mores to live by, rituals to perform, and doctrines to assent to.

This is how many Christians operate. They see the Bible as a book of doctrine that informs their code of ethics and attending worship services as their obligatory weekly ritual. Is this religious routine really all there is? Is this the point of our faith?

The truth is, we know there is something more. We were created to be in the very presence of God Himself. What if God is actually available to us now? If we truly believe this, how might it color how we live?

Take a moment to read through the Scriptures on pages 12-13 before watching "Presence of God" (12:50). Then discuss the two questions designed as follow-up to the video on the Viewer Guide page.

SHOW VIDEO NOW.

VIEWER GUIDE

Included are two questions designed as follow-up to "Presence of God." This time is set aside for discussion within the group about what they heard, how it affected them, and possible applications. These questions may be only a beginning. Feel free to begin the conversation by asking what thoughts, insights, or stories had the most impact on group members.

> **"Presence is the point of Christianity. ... Having the presence of God in our lives has *always* been the point."**

1. J.D. talks passionately in his video message about how the point of the Exodus was so that Israel might *know* God (Exodus 8:1). How does J.D. define "know" in this context?

   ❑ know many facts about ❑ understand deeply
   ❑ like a friend ❑ personal
   ❑ intimate ❑ other: _____

2. According to J.D., what is it that makes the Bible's approach to "knowing" and "doing" different from other religions?

BIBLICAL BACKGROUND

With music there is usually a story behind the song that helps listeners appreciate the heart and soul behind both the music and the lyrics. Scripture is no different. Below you'll find a brief story behind this week's Scripture intended to provide additional understanding and insight.

The Book of Exodus tells the story of God freeing Israel from Egypt's captivity so that they can worship Him in the place He has set aside for worship. Exodus 33 documents a fascinating conversation between God and Moses. Throughout the conversation we see Moses interceding for Israel and God showing mercy and compassion. At the key point of the conversation, Moses rejects God's offer to bless Israel with prosperity because God says He will not send His presence with them. Moses would rather be in the desert with God's presence than in the promised land without it.

In John 14, Jesus affirms that the same presence of God which was with Moses and Israel, which was embodied in Christ, will now dwell within every Christian in the form of God's Holy Spirit. We see a continuation of the reality that God's presence is the only thing humanity needs.

SCRIPTURE

³ "Go up to a land flowing with milk and honey. But I will not go with you because you are a stiff-necked people; otherwise, I might destroy you on the way." ... ¹⁵ "If Your presence does not go," Moses responded to Him, "don't make us go up from here. ¹⁶ How will it be known that I and Your people have found favor in Your sight unless You go with us? I and Your people will be distinguished by this from all the other people on the face of the earth."

¹⁷ The LORD answered Moses, "I will do this very thing you have asked, for you have found favor in My sight, and I know you by name." ¹⁸ Then Moses said, "Please, let me see Your glory." – Exodus 33:3,15-18

Then the man and his wife heard the sound of the LORD God walking in the garden at the time of the evening breeze, and they hid themselves from the LORD God among the trees of the garden. – Genesis 3:8

¹⁵ If you love Me, you will keep My commands. ¹⁶ And I will ask the Father, and He will give you another Counselor to be with you forever. ¹⁷ He is the Spirit of truth. The world is unable to receive Him because it doesn't see Him or know Him. But you do know Him, because He remains with you and will be in you. – John 14:15-17

I greatly rejoice in the Lord, I exult in my God; for He has clothed me with the garments of salvation and wrapped me in a robe of righteousness, as a groom wears a turban and as a bride adorns herself with her jewels. – Isaiah 61:10

[15] For you did not receive a spirit of slavery to fall back into fear, but you received the Spirit of adoption, by whom we cry out, "Abba, Father!" [16] The Spirit Himself testifies together with our spirit that we are God's children, [17] and if children, also heirs—heirs of God and co-heirs with Christ—seeing that we suffer with Him so that we may also be glorified with Him. – Romans 8:15-17

[37] In all these things we are more than victorious through Him who loved us. [38] For I am persuaded that not even death or life, angels or rulers, things present or things to come, hostile powers, [39] height or depth, or any other created thing will have the power to separate us from the love of God that is in Christ Jesus our Lord! – Romans 8:37-39

SMALL-GROUP QUESTIONS

Over the next few pages you'll find discussion questions, material that may be used as additional discussion points, and a journal exercise for group members to complete away from the group.

"What if God promised all the blessings of life to you—a good marriage, good health, good family, even to take you to heaven when you die—but He Himself, His presence, would not go with you on the way? Would that be OK with you?"

1. Look back at the conversation between Moses and God in Exodus 33:17-18. Which of the phrases that describe the relationship between God and Moses is most powerful to you? Explain.

2. Moses seems desperate for God's presence. What does this tell us about the distinction that separates God's people from others?

WELL SAID

"The Lord Jesus is in the midst of His Church. Not physically, but still in real truth, Jesus is with us. And a blessed truth it is, for where Jesus is, love becomes inflamed. Of all the things in the world that can set the heart burning, there is nothing like the presence of Jesus! A glimpse of Him so overcomes us that we are ready to say 'Turn away your eyes from me for they have overcome me.'

"If we know that Jesus is with us, every power will be developed and every grace will be strengthened, and we shall cast ourselves into the Lord's service with heart and soul and strength; therefore is the presence of Christ to be desired above all things." [1] — Charles Spurgeon

"The human condition is one of nakedness."

3. The center of the gospel is that Jesus came to restore the relationship between man and God. How does the gospel heal the human condition of nakedness?

4. After the fall, Adam and Eve realized their nakedness and hid from the presence of the Lord. Sin made them aware and ashamed of their nakedness before God. Adam and Eve were literally naked. In what ways are we figuratively naked?

"It's not simply what we believe. It's not simply how we live. What sets us apart is the fact that the presence of God is with us. ... Is that what you are known for?"

5. Romans 8:37-39 promises that Christians cannot be separated from the love of Christ. How could this intersect with the need for the presence of God in our lives?

6. How does Romans 8:15-17 give further understanding about how the presence of God impacts our lives?

"I AM YOUR FATHER"

Perhaps one of the most quoted lines in cinematic history comes from the epic movie series *Star Wars*. In Episode V, *The Empire Strikes Back*, Luke confronts and accuses Darth Vader of killing his father. Vader responds with the famous line, "No, *I* am your father." This information colors the rest of Luke's journey.

While the overarching story is a cosmic good and evil battle, there is a very strong subplot of Luke seeking to avenge the loss of his father. All of a sudden, he is reunited with the father he thought he had lost forever. This changes Luke.

Though Vader is the second most powerful villain in the universe, the love for his father and desire for a relationship with him compels Luke not to kill Vader when he has the chance.

Regardless of your personal experience with a parent or child, this portrayal taps the deep human reality that we long for a relationship with a father. We were created for it.

JOURNAL

This journaling opportunity is designed for group members to utilize at another time. They may choose to answer the questions in the space provided or they may prefer to use the space and time to take a deep question or concern to God.

> **"What we lost when we were cast out of the garden of Eden was God's presence. And so that's what our hearts have always yearned for—to know God again, to be reunited to Him, to have Him again be our Father and our Friend."**

The gospel is not about what you can do to make God love you, but what He has done *because* He loves you. How do you perceive your relationship with God right now? How does this new understanding of the need for His presence challenge you?

YOU'RE UP

To put into practice the lessons from God's Word in this session, keep the following things in mind:

- Think about the most stressful area of your life right now. Ask God to help you understand and experience how His presence can bring you peace in this area.

- Tell one other group member which area you chose and ask him or her to follow up with you during the week or the next time the group gathers.

- Write down any Scripture passages or insights from your study this week that reminded you of your need for the presence of God in your life. Come ready to share with the group next time.

In the next session we will look at understanding more of what the presence of God looks like in our lives. To prepare for the lesson, take a few minutes to read Exodus 34:5-9; Acts 2:43-47; and 1 Corinthians 14:24-25.

1. Charles H. Spurgeon, *Strengthen My Spirit* (Uhrichsville, OH: Barbour Publishing, Inc., 2011), 46.

Experiencing God

A walk through a Christian bookstore, or any bookstore really, will reveal that we are not short on opportunities to access knowledge about God. We have everything from dense systematic theologies to on-the-go devotionals to exhaustive commentaries. We can play Bible trivia games online or with our friends. We can participate in a wide range of programs at church designed to help the whole family learn more of the Bible. While these things are certainly not bad, they can carry a subtle danger.

We can become a community of people content to learn facts about God instead of seeking to know God Himself. The Bible mentions a group of people like this—the Pharisees. These religious leaders knew more about God than anyone in their time. Yet their hearts had grown cold to experiencing God. Their religious doctrine crowded out their relationship with the God they claimed to serve.

Is this us?

WARM UP

Try not to spend too much time here, but let everyone answer the warm-up question. Getting group members involved early helps create the best small-group environment.

If you got to select the category for your final question on the popular trivia show "Jeopardy," what would you choose?

❑ Word Origins   ❑ American History
❑ State Capitals   ❑ World Geography
❑ Sports   ❑ Animals
❑ US Cities   ❑ Pop Music
❑ Literature   ❑ Shakespeare
❑ US Presidents   ❑ Authors
❑ Famous Americans   ❑ Other: _____

Explain your answer.

VIDEO SET UP

The information below sets up the video. It can be read aloud to the group, read by group members ahead of time, or group members can read the information silently while the facilitator sets up the video.

We crave answers. Reason and logic dominate not just our intellectual side but also our emotional and relational sides. When something happens, we are conditioned to ask why. We come to God with our rational framework. We look at the Bible as a formula to decipher in order to build a proper knowledge of God. And accurate knowledge is vital. God must be known as He revealed Himself in His Word.

We also crave experiences. We want to be swept up into something beyond ourselves that gives us a taste of the grandeur of life we know must be out there. So we crave an experience with God that is actually beyond our comprehension.

What if what we find in the presence of God is the ultimate place where truth and experience meet?

In this session we are going to look at the anatomy of the presence of God. What is it? What does it look like for us in the 21st century? How is this different from the imitation brand of presence we have conjured up to fit our religious experience?

Take a moment to read through the Scripture passages on pages 26-27 before watching "Experiencing God" (11:04). Then discuss the two questions designed as follow-up to the video on the Viewer Guide page.

SHOW VIDEO NOW.

VIEWER GUIDE

Included are two questions designed as follow-up to "Experiencing God." This time is set aside for discussion within the group about what they heard, how it affected them, and possible applications. These questions may be only a beginning. Feel free to begin the conversation by asking what thoughts, insights, or stories had the most impact on group members.

1. In the video message, J.D. says, "It's possible to be very blessed and to live completely apart from the presence of God." What do you think he means by that?

2. How does J.D. define the presence of God?

BIBLICAL BACKGROUND

With music there is usually a story behind the song that helps listeners appreciate the heart and soul behind both the music and the lyrics. Scripture is no different. Below you'll find a brief story behind this week's Scripture intended to provide additional understanding and insight.

One of the clear themes of Scripture is that God is not a distant ruler but instead a Father who chooses to remain deeply involved in the lives of His children. And when He makes His presence known among His people, everything else fades into the background.

In Exodus 34 God presents Himself to Moses by declaring His name to him. Moses later comes off the mountain radiating from the encounter. In Deuteronomy 6 God teaches Israel how to keep their love of Him as the central focus of their lives—by remembering His words and His name.

Jesus teaches in John 14 about the Holy Spirit, the presence of God, and how it will literally dwell in His followers. We see in Acts 2 how the entire community was in awe of the power of God present among the early church. And 1 Corinthians 14 shows us how a healthy church will worship together in such a way that unbelievers will experience the presence of God.

In all of these texts, we see the centrality of the presence of God *among* His people and the power of God at work *through* His people by their faith in His revealed name.

SCRIPTURE

⁵ The LORD came down in a cloud, stood with him there, and proclaimed His name Yahweh. ⁶ Then the LORD passed in front of him and proclaimed: Yahweh—Yahweh is a compassionate and gracious God, slow to anger and rich in faithful love and truth, ⁷ maintaining faithful love to a thousand generations, forgiving wrongdoing, rebellion, and sin. But He will not leave the guilty unpunished, bringing the consequences of the fathers' wrongdoing on the children and grandchildren to the third and fourth generation.

⁸ Moses immediately bowed down to the ground and worshiped. ⁹ Then he said, "My Lord, if I have indeed found favor in Your sight, my Lord, please go with us. Even though this is a stiff-necked people, forgive our wrongdoing and sin, and accept us as Your own possession." – Exodus 34:5-9

¹⁵ If you love Me, you will keep My commands. ¹⁶ And I will ask the Father, and He will give you another Counselor to be with you forever. ¹⁷ He is the Spirit of truth. The world is unable to receive Him because it doesn't see Him or know Him. But you do know Him, because He remains with you and will be in you. ¹⁸ I will not leave you as orphans; I am coming to you. – John 14:15-18

[43] Then fear came over everyone, and many wonders and signs were being performed through the apostles. [44] Now all the believers were together and held all things in common. [45] They sold their possessions and property and distributed the proceeds to all, as anyone had a need. [46] Every day they devoted themselves to meeting together in the temple complex, and broke bread from house to house. They ate their food with a joyful and humble attitude, [47] praising God and having favor with all the people. And every day the Lord added to them those who were being saved. – Acts 2:43-47

[24] If all are prophesying and some unbeliever or uninformed person comes in, he is convicted by all and is judged by all. [25] The secrets of his heart will be revealed, and as a result he will fall facedown and worship God, proclaiming, "God is really among you." – 1 Corinthians 14:24-25

SMALL-GROUP QUESTIONS

Over the next few pages you'll find discussion questions, material that may be used as additional discussion points, and a journal exercise for group members to complete away from the group.

> **"Presence is an immediate, first-hand heart sense of the size, the character, and the attributes of God. ... I want people who are overwhelmed by a sense of guilt for their problems to suddenly come in and be more overwhelmed by a sense of the size of God's grace and how much bigger He is than all of the universe."**

1. Have you ever felt completely overwhelmed? So filled with emotion your brain can't figure out how to respond, leaving your body to either weep or leap with joy? What details can you remember about the occasion?

2. John 14:15-18 reveals that as Christians, the Spirit of Truth will always be in us. How do you think this affects how we experience God?

3. Based on John 14:15-18, how do you think the Holy Spirit helps us sense the presence of God in our lives?

A NEW REALITY

In the cult classic *The Matrix,* Keanu Reeves begins the story as a rather mundane systems analyst named Thomas Anderson. He is not satisfied with his life and spends his off-work time searching for meaning beyond his job. When a curious character named Morpheus leads Anderson to experience a new reality outside of "the matrix" he's been trapped in, everything changes. Anderson, now called Neo, begins to operate in the matrix with a new sense of freedom and confidence like he never had before. Experiencing a new reality gives Neo an entirely new set of eyes with which to see his prior context. When we step into the presence of God, our perception of the world and our lives change forever.

> **"What is the presence of God? It is a first-hand heart knowledge of the name of God, His character, His size, the immensity of His love."**

4. In his book *Knowing God*, J.I. Packer wrote, "We must seek, in studying God, to be led to God. It was for this purpose that revelation was given, and it is to this use that we must put it." [1] How would you define a healthy balance between knowing about God and truly knowing God?

> **"What we have are people who are educated but not bold because they have knowledge and not presence."**

5. In both Acts 2 and 1 Corinthians 14, unbelievers encounter a healthy body of believers and are transformed. How is the presence of God connected to the community of God? What does this mean for you and your small group?

MOURNING WITH HOPE

When my wife and I (Spence) lost our third child to a miscarriage, we were devastated. The pain of the loss and the lingering desire for an explanation from God flooded our lives for a period of time. We never doubted our theology, but in many ways we experienced our theology for the first time.

First Thessalonians 4:13-14 was a passage we clung to. It tells us that we grieve not as those with no hope. It tells us that because Christ has defeated death, we know He takes those who have fallen asleep with Him.

It's not that this became more true to us, but that it became a firsthand source of joy instead of a distant doctrine. That "the sufferings of this present time are not worth comparing with the glory that is going to be revealed to us" (Romans 8:18) is not just something we know but something we cling to.

The presence of God met us in our desperation. Our theology never changed, but our awareness of our daily need for God's presence changed forever.

JOURNAL

This journaling opportunity is designed for group members to utilize at another time. They may choose to answer the questions in the space provided or they may prefer to use the space and time to take a deep question or concern to God.

"To be in a place of presence we have to have our minds full of the Word of God and our hearts full of the Spirit of God."

"If you have the Spirit without the Word, you blow up. If you have the Word without the Spirit, you dry up. But you get the Word and the Spirit together, and you grow up."

Usually we fall victim to overemphasizing either the Word of God or the Spirit of God in our walk with Christ. If you had to give an honest evaluation of your relationship to God right now, which would you say you tend to lean toward? How can what you've learned about the presence of God help you grow from where you are right now?

YOU'RE UP

As you meditate on God's presence and what it looks like in your life, take the following points as a challenge to consider this week:

- Think about the last time you were sincerely overwhelmed by God's mercy. Take some time to meditate on what that means for your life now.

- While you probably will not see God's presence in a cloud like Moses did, evidences of His presence in your life are all around. Take note this week of what you read in Scripture and see in life that leads you to say, "God is really here."

- Come ready to share at least one evidence of God's presence in your life the next time your group gathers.

In the next session we will look at how we can fulfill our desire to truly experience the presence of God in our lives. To prepare for the lesson, take a few minutes to read Exodus 33:4-11 and John 1:17-18.

1. J.I. Packer, *Knowing God* (Downers Grove, IL: InterVarsity Press, 1993), 8.

Finding God

Desire is one of the most intense human emotions. It has led people to great acts of evil and great acts of good. Desire drives us all. We desire things like a spouse, a dream job, a family, and then we work hard to get them. We seek, and can often find, instruction on how to get what we desire. We take courses, read books, and consult experts to help us on our quest to acquire the target of our desire.

Whether we know it or not, our hearts are designed for God. We have a hunger only He can fill. We search for Him even in the darkness of our sin.

Is there a way for this, the most intense of all desires, to be realized? How can we fulfill our desire to step into the presence of God?

WARM UP

Try not to spend too much time here, but let everyone answer the warm-up questions. Getting group members involved early helps create the best small-group environment.

Think of a toy, game, or object that you wanted more than anything as a child. Did you get it? How?

As an adult, has there been a job you landed, position you achieved, or event you experienced because you were driven by a strong desire for it? What did you go through to get this thing you desired so much?

VIDEO SET UP

The information below sets up the video. It can be read aloud to the group, read by group members ahead of time, or group members can read the information silently while the facilitator sets up the video.

Christians have practiced many rituals to try and draw close to God. The building of the great cathedrals across Europe were an attempt to create a space worthy of the presence of God. The isolation found in the monasteries was believed to allow monks to more easily commune with God. Holy water was and still is used to purify oneself to be worthy to stand before God.

Prayer vigils are held in hopes of speaking to and being heard by God. Music is created to bring out in us a full expression of worship to God. Christians paid indulgences in medieval times to secure the presence of God for their deceased relatives.

We want to find and keep the presence of God in our lives. But is there a special formula that will allow us to enter into and remain in the presence of God? And how is Jesus involved in all of this? In this session J.D. will explore these things.

Take a moment to read through the Scripture passages on page 40 before watching "Finding God" (16:29). Then discuss the two questions designed as follow up to the video on the Viewer Guide page.

SHOW VIDEO NOW.

VIEWER GUIDE

Included are two questions designed as follow-up to "Finding God." This time is set aside for discussion within the group about what they heard, how it affected them, and possible applications. These questions may be only a beginning. Feel free to begin the conversation by asking what thoughts, insights, or stories had the most impact on group members.

1. What are the three things we can do to experience the presence of God?

2. According to J.D.'s message, what is the greatest gift we can give another person?

BIBLICAL BACKGROUND

With music there is usually a story behind the song that helps listeners appreciate the heart and soul behind both the music and the lyrics. Scripture is no different. Below you'll find a brief story behind this week's Scripture intended to provide additional understanding and insight.

The apostle Paul didn't have it easy. He was beaten, mocked, threatened, imprisoned, and scorned by society for virtually all of his time in ministry. But in the thick of that suffering, Paul kept a very diligent, rich prayer life. Paul's letters are inundated with prayer for his readers in the beginning, middle, and end. Paul understood prayer to be his lifeline to the power of God and so he counseled the believers to pray continually.

He knew the main thing that would keep believers from real prayer would be their idolatry and their religion. So he pleaded with them to throw off their old ways and habits of sin and live as people who had the presence of God, just like God called the Israelites to do when He rebuked them for worshiping the golden calf.

Paul counseled believers against replacing the gospel they believed in with religious duties. Paul prayed for God to give the believers more of Jesus. He knew the greatest thing we need is God Himself, and that only comes through the reconciling death of Jesus.

SCRIPTURE

⁵ The LORD said to Moses: "Tell the Israelites: You are a stiff-necked people. If I went with you for a single moment, I would destroy you. Now take off your jewelry, and I will decide what to do with you." ... ⁷ Now Moses took a tent and set it up outside the camp, far away from the camp; he called it the tent of meeting. Anyone who wanted to consult the LORD would go to the tent of meeting. ... ¹¹ Then Moses would return to the camp, but his assistant, the young man Joshua son of Nun, would not leave the inside of the tent. – Exodus 33:5,7,11

¹⁷ For the law was given through Moses, grace and truth came through Jesus Christ. ¹⁸ No one has ever seen God. The One and Only Son—the One who is at the Father's side—He has revealed Him. – John 1:17-18

I only want to learn this from you: Did you receive the Spirit by the works of the law or by hearing with faith?
– Galatians 3:2

¹⁶ I pray that He may grant you, according to the riches of His glory, to be strengthened with power in the inner man through His Spirit, ¹⁷ and that the Messiah may dwell in your hearts through faith. I pray that you, being rooted and firmly established in love, ¹⁸ may be able to comprehend with all the saints what is the length and width, height and depth of God's love, ¹⁹ and to know the Messiah's love that surpasses knowledge, so you may be filled with all the fullness of God. – Ephesians 3:16-19

SMALL-GROUP QUESTIONS

Over the next few pages you'll find discussion questions, material that may be used as additional discussion points, and a journal exercise for group members to complete away from the group.

> **"When you pray, what are you most praying for? ... The greatest gift that you could ever give to anybody is your intimacy with God."**

1. Look at the Ephesians 3 passage. What do you learn about Paul through his prayer for the believers in Ephesus?

2. How do you think our intimacy with God should, or could, change the way we pray?

WELL SAID

"The presence of God is not the same as the *sense* of the presence of God. ... The real parallel on the natural level is one which seems odd for a bachelor to write to a lady, but too illuminating not to be used. The act which engenders a child ought to be, and usually is, attended by pleasure. But it is not the pleasure that produces the child. Where there is pleasure there may be sterility: where there is no pleasure the act may be fertile. And in the spiritual marriage of God and the soul it is the same. It is the actual presence, not the *sensation* of the presence, of the Holy Ghost which begets Christ in us. The *sense* of the presence is a super-added gift for which we give thanks when it comes, and that's all about it."[1] — C.S. Lewis, 1955

"If there's one thing that we have perfected, it is the art of the instant world. ... If you are going to be filled with the presence of God, it's going to take time."

3. What are some ways the desire for the "instant world" has crept into our lives with Christ?

4. What is key in fighting against this temptation?

"You cannot have God and hang on to sin."

5. In Exodus 33, God required the Israelites to take off their ornaments as an outward sign of the genuine repentance going on in their hearts. When we really do want God's presence, why do you think it's sometimes so hard for us to let go of our sin?

6. What are a couple of practical steps your small group could take to help one another combat the sin that is keeping you from experiencing the presence of God?

"I know His presence is in my life not because I am better than you, but simply because I have received what God has offered me in Christ."

7. In Galatians 3:2, Paul reminds the Galatians that it was by faith alone they received the presence of God in their lives. When it comes to believing the gospel and following Christ, where are you in your life right now?

PRAYER IN A HAYSTACK

In 1806 at Williams College in Massachusetts, a tiny band of five students were looking for a place to pray. The hostility toward Christians on campus was so intense they felt afraid to pray on campus and even kept the minutes of their meetings hidden. So they went off campus to a nearby farm to pray for revival at their school. When a storm broke out, they burrowed under a haystack for protection and continued to pray.

A revival came to Williams College not long afterward, and with it a powerful world missions movement. The youthful leader of that prayer group, Samuel Mills, would later become one of the founders of the American Board of Commissioners for Foreign Missions and the American Bible Society. [2]

Today there is a plaque on the site with the inscription: The Birthplace of American Foreign Missions.

JOURNAL

This journaling opportunity is designed for group members to utilize at another time. They may choose to answer the question in the space provided or they may prefer to use the space and time to take a deep question or concern to God.

> "What is it that fills you with the Spirit?
> Believing the gospel! ...
> You want to be filled more with the presence of God?
> Be filled more with the mind of Christ."

Much like an athlete needs constant exercise to stay in shape, so a believer needs to constantly consider and believe the good news of Jesus Christ's death and resurrection. When you think about that good news, how does it connect to the various areas of your life today? Take some time to consider and write down how the gospel was not just news you heard once but news you still need to believe in your life today.

YOU'RE UP

As you consider how you can find and experience the presence of God, go over the points below which are intended to push you deeper into God's presence throughout this week:

- For most people, their prayer life is the first thing to fade into the background when life's pace quickens around them. How would you characterize your time in prayer lately? (Remember that the goal here is not guilt. The goal is connecting prayer to the joy found in God's presence.)

- Take an honest assessment of your daily routine and ask yourself: *Is there anything captivating me more than God and His gospel right now?* If there is, spend some time examining what those things are.

- Come ready next week to share at least one way you are trying to believe and live out the gospel in your everyday routine.

Next session we will look at what to do when it feels like God is silent. To prepare for the lesson, take a few minutes to read Exodus 32:21-24,31-32.

1. C.S. Lewis, *Yours, Jack* (New York, NY: HarperCollins Publishers, 2008), 257.
2. "Samuel J. Mills," *Williams College: Archives and Special Collections* [online], [cited 20 May 2011]. Available on the Internet: *http://archives.williams.edu/williamshistory/biographies/mills-samuel-j.php.*

Fear and God

One of the most captivating of all human experiences is fear. Whether physical, financial, or emotional, fear sells. Reality TV's popularity is fueled by our desire to see how real people deal with real fear. Heroes are not made on the golf channel, after all; they are made in the line of fire. We love the story of the underdog who makes it to the top because we can empathize in some way with their fear. And we find hope in his or her success. Fear reveals our deepest nature.

Life presents much to fear. Stress, worry, and anxiety are all products of our fear of the unknown. Who knows what tomorrow brings? Surely God has given us a way to process it all.

WARM UP

Try not to spend too much time here, but let everyone answer the warm-up questions. Getting group members involved early helps create the best small-group environment.

Thinking back to your childhood, who was your favorite hero?

What big fear did you overcome growing up—riding a bike, learning to swim, going to 6th grade because you were obviously uncool (Oh wait, that was just me.), and so on?

VIDEO SET UP

The information below sets up the video. It can be read aloud to the group, read by group members ahead of time, or group members can read the information silently while the facilitator sets up the video.

While TV shows and movies resolve difficult dilemmas in an hour or two, real life is not so easy. Everyone, at some point or another, will deal with pain and hardship. The question is not *if* a difficult time will come, but *when*. When it comes, how will you respond?

The insurance industry makes billions annually off of this question. Self-help remedies, life coaches, and religious institutions are also big industries because they offer their own answers. But where do we turn when life gets really rough?

In this session we are going to see Israel's true colors revealed at the foot of the very mountain where their God was residing. Pay special attention to how God teaches them to deal with the fear of the unknown.

Take a moment to read through the Scripture passages on pages 54-55 before watching "Fear and God" (12:07). Then discuss the two questions designed as follow-up to the video on the Viewer Guide page.

SHOW VIDEO NOW.

VIEWER GUIDE

Included are two questions designed as follow-up to "Fear and God." This time is set aside for discussion within the group about what they heard, how it affected them, and possible applications. These questions may be only a beginning. Feel free to begin the conversation by asking what thoughts, insights, or stories had the most impact on group members.

1. In his video message, J.D. draws a parallel between the first sin with Adam and Eve and what the Israelites did at Mount Horeb with the golden calf. What are some similarities in their reactions?

2. What is the point of J.D.'s marble illustration?

BIBLICAL BACKGROUND

With music there is usually a story behind the song that helps listeners appreciate the heart and soul behind both the music and the lyrics. Scripture is no different. Below you'll find a brief story behind this week's Scripture intended to provide additional understanding and insight.

Trusting in the Lord is one of the most frequently taught and repeated principles in all of Scripture. It is at the very core of Christian belief and is the base-level prescription for every element of our lives. The basic story of the Old Testament is Israel trusting in something other than God, God correcting them, and their repentance to and worship of their Savior King.

The New Testament is no different. At its core is Jesus calling a people to trust in Him as their new way of life. To rest, or abide, in His love for them and allow their lives to bear fruit for God's glory. The apostle Paul's teaching on how to live as a Christian is, at its core, simply applying the love of the gospel to every area of life.

Both Jesus and Paul caution believers against fear and anxiety by reminding them that everything they need has already been provided by God. Paul can "rejoice" because his deepest needs were met in Jesus' death and resurrection. When we replace worry with God's love, we begin to overflow with the power of hope abiding in us.

SCRIPTURE

²¹ Then Moses asked Aaron, "What did these people do to you that you have led them into such a grave sin?" ²² "Don't be enraged, my lord," Aaron replied. "You yourself know that the people are intent on evil. ²³ They said to me, 'Make us a god who will go before us because this Moses, the man who brought us up from the land of Egypt—we don't know what has happened to him!' ²⁴ So I said to them, 'Whoever has gold, take it off,' and they gave it to me. When I threw it into the fire, out came this calf!" ... ³¹ So Moses returned to the LORD and said, "Oh, these people have committed a grave sin; they have made a god of gold for themselves. ³² Now if You would only forgive their sin. But if not, please erase me from the book You have written." – Exodus 32:21-24,31-32

Anxiety in a man's heart weighs it down, but a good word cheers it up. – Proverbs 12:25

⁴ Rejoice in the Lord always. I will say it again: Rejoice! ⁵ Let your graciousness be known to everyone. The Lord is near. ⁶ Don't worry about anything, but in everything, through prayer and petition with thanksgiving, let your requests be made known to God. ⁷ And the peace of God, which surpasses every thought, will guard your hearts and minds in Christ Jesus. – Philippians 4:4-7

[31] So don't worry, saying, "What will we eat?" or "What will we drink?" or "What will we wear?" [32] For the idolaters eagerly seek all these things, and your heavenly Father knows that you need them. [33] But seek first the kingdom of God and His righteousness, and all these things will be provided for you. – Matthew 6:31-33

[5] I am the vine; you are the branches. The one who remains in Me and I in him produces much fruit, because you can do nothing without Me. [6] If anyone does not remain in Me, he is thrown aside like a branch and he withers. They gather them, throw them into the fire, and they are burned. [7] If you remain in Me and My words remain in you, ask whatever you want and it will be done for you. [8] My Father is glorified by this: that you produce much fruit and prove to be My disciples. – John 15:5-8

[2] Like newborn infants, desire the pure spiritual milk, so that you may grow by it for your salvation, [3] since you have tasted that the Lord is good. [4] Coming to Him, a living stone—rejected by men but chosen and valuable to God— [5] you yourselves, as living stones, are being built into a spiritual house for a holy priesthood to offer spiritual sacrifices acceptable to God through Jesus Christ. – 1 Peter 2:2-5

Now may the God of hope fill you with all joy and peace as you believe in Him so that you may overflow with hope by the power of the Holy Spirit. – Romans 15:13

SMALL-GROUP QUESTIONS

Over the next few pages you'll find discussion questions, material that may be used as additional discussion points, and a journal exercise for group members to complete away from the group.

"In times of stress, fear, or worry, we return to the gods in which we are most familiar trusting."

1. What lies did the Israelites believe that led them down the road to worshiping a golden calf?

2. The Israelites didn't renounce God; they supplemented Him. What do you tend to trust in addition to God? About what do you think, "I know I need God, but I also need _____ for life to be OK?

3. *Sanctification* is the process of putting our old lives behind and becoming more like Christ. What do you think putting away comfort zones, fears, and would-be security blankets has to do with sanctification (John 15 and 1 Peter 2)?

RUDY! RUDY! RUDY!

In 1993 Sean Astin played the role of Daniel 'Rudy' Ruettiger in *Rudy*. The movie is based on the true story of an undersized Midwestern son of a steel mill worker. He dreamed of playing football for Notre Dame, the most prestigious football program in the country at the time.

It took four tries for Rudy to get into Notre Dame. Once in, it took him many more tries to even get on the practice squad of the mighty fighting Irish. The movie ends with Rudy dressing out and getting to play a couple of plays at the end of the game.

When obstacle after obstacle got in the way, Rudy kept his eyes and heart focused on his desire to run onto the field as a player for his dream school.

Rudy's goal pushed him through the obstacles that made it seem impossible for him to ever play for Notre Dame. How much more then can we, as Christians who have the hope and vision of heaven, face the fears and uncertainties of life?

"Which unanswered prayers in your life have really bothered you?"

4. Look at Philippians 4:4-7 and describe in your words the approach to prayer Paul is exhorting his readers to take.

5. How can the peace of God meet us and give us hope in times of pain and adversity?

6. The command in Matthew 6:33 seems simple enough— "seek first the kingdom of God." But why, in your opinion, does following it seem so difficult, especially during stressful times?

"Life's knocks don't create the problem, they just reveal it."

7. Anxiety is always creeping around the corner. What does your reaction to "life's knocks" reveal about the way you process the world around you? How could becoming more aware of these tendencies contribute to your spiritual growth?

8. What steps can you take today to reclaim the peace and hope of God in your life?

IN THE FACE OF FEAR: "YES"

Anyone old enough to remember April 20, 1999 recalls sitting in shock as the news out of Columbine High School began rolling across TV screens around the country. The deadliest massacre in American education history at that time ended in 12 students and one teacher dead with dozens of others wounded.

One of those students, Cassie Bernall, was hiding under a desk when a gunman confronted her with the question, "Do you believe in God?" With only a second to think, she replied, "Yes." A split second later the gunman shot and killed her.

Cassie didn't plan on being given a life-and-death ultimatum that day. When crisis struck, this 17-year-old revealed what was already inside of her—a love and devotion to her God.

JOURNAL

This journaling opportunity is designed for group members to utilize at another time. They may choose to answer the questions in the space provided or they may prefer to use the space and time to take a deep question or concern to God.

> **"Where does the trail of your worry, your fear, your stress ... lead back to? These are your idolatries. ... What is still inside of you?"**

What habits, relationships, and/or ways of relating to the world could be keeping you from experiencing the presence of God in your life? In other words, what areas of sin in your life are functioning as idols? Take some time to reflect and consider this question before you respond.

YOU'RE UP

Throughout this week you will have plenty of opportunities to get stressed, worried, or anxious about things. Instead of reacting to those situations, consider the following as a challenge to help you proactively live in the peace of God:

- Use your daily commute as a time to execute Paul's call to rejoice in your identity in Christ.

- Write down every promise you've been given from God that you come across as you read Scripture.

- Rest. Not sleep, not recreation, not mindless TV watching, but rest. Sit before God. Give His peace the opportunity to wash over you.

- Come next week ready to share with the group what you took away from your week with God.

Next week we will look at what it feels like when God seems absent from our lives. To prepare for the lesson, take a few minutes to reread Exodus 32:21-24,31-32. You might also want to look at John 1:1-5; 3:19-21; Matthew 28:18-20; Deuteronomy 6:10-12; and Hebrews 11:1-3.

When God Seems Silent

Have you ever felt like God wasn't listening to you? Like your prayers were falling on deaf ears? Like your fear of being utterly alone was actually coming true? Sometimes this feeling occurs in the monotony of a life we suddenly aren't sure how we ended up in. Sometimes it's in the throes of a relationship catastrophe. We feel it when disaster, man-made or natural, strikes our world.

In these dark moments, we feel abandoned by the God we thought loved us and cared for us. If this has ever described you, you are not alone. None of us feel the presence of God in our lives all the time. Did you do something wrong? Did God give up on you? It is easy to allow doubt, confusion, and frustration to seep into our lives and consume our thoughts when the God we rely on seems nowhere to be found. What do we do when heaven seems silent?

WARM UP

Try not to spend too much time here, but let everyone answer the warm-up questions. Getting group members involved early helps create the best small-group environment.

In our world of GPS technology, the possibility of being completely lost is far less than it used to be. Have you ever been completely lost or disoriented—as a child or as an adult? Describe what being lost felt like.

How did you feel when you finally got your bearings?

VIDEO SET UP

The information below sets up the video. It can be read aloud to the group, read by group members ahead of time, or group members can read the information silently while the facilitator sets up the video.

Faith is the soil of Christianity. But what *is* faith? Is it a synonym for belief or hope? Merely wishful thinking? An assent to a set of doctrines? Hebrews 11:1 tells us, "Faith is the reality of what is hoped for, the proof of what is not seen." Faith provides confidence in the midst of uncertainty. Faith is to the Christian what an anchor is to a ship.

In this session, J.D. picks up where he left off last time talking about how we respond to adversity and fear as God's people. This session will specifically look at how the promises of God sustain us when we can't find God. Leaders, this session will be particularly important for you as J.D. teaches from Aaron's mistakes on some core leadership principles for anyone in Christian leadership.

Take a moment to read through the Scripture passages on pages 68-69 before watching "When God Seems Silent" (15:49). Then discuss the two questions designed as follow-up to the video on the Viewer Guide page.

SHOW VIDEO NOW.

VIEWER GUIDE

Included are two questions designed as follow-up to "When God Seems Silent." This time is set aside for discussion within the group about what they heard, how it affected them, and possible applications. These questions may be only a beginning. Feel free to begin the conversation by asking what thoughts, insights, or stories had the most impact on group members.

1. When we feel like God is absent, what does J.D. say assures us that He is not?

2. What are some practical ways to keep the Word of God in front of us?

BIBLICAL BACKGROUND

With music there is usually a story behind the song that helps listeners appreciate the heart and soul behind both the music and the lyrics. Scripture is no different. Below you'll find a brief story behind this week's Scripture intended to provide additional understanding and insight.

The power of light to penetrate darkness is truly remarkable. The human eye can see a lit candle in the midst of darkness from miles away. The contrast between light and darkness is one of the richest, most frequently used metaphors in Scripture. It represents the battle between good and evil.

In Scripture, darkness represents evil, temptation, sin, and suffering. The Gospel of John introduces Jesus as the light from heaven, piercing the darkness. His light expelled the darkness in our lives.

The Scriptures teach us that faith, or the certain conviction of the yet unseen promises of God, is the medium by which we access this light during dark times in our lives. We remember that Christ has promised to remain with us, His disciples, until the very end of the world when He is going to then reign in person as our Forever King.

SCRIPTURE

²¹ Then Moses asked Aaron, "What did these people do to you that you have led them into such a grave sin?" ²² "Don't be enraged, my lord," Aaron replied. "You yourself know that the people are intent on evil. ²³ They said to me, 'Make us a god who will go before us because this Moses, the man who brought us up from the land of Egypt—we don't know what has happened to him!' ²⁴ So I said to them, 'Whoever has gold, take it off,' and they gave it to me. When I threw it into the fire, out came this calf!" ... ³¹ So Moses returned to the LORD and said, "Oh, these people have committed a grave sin; they have made a god of gold for themselves. ³² Now if You would only forgive their sin. But if not, please erase me from the book You have written." – Exodus 32:21-24,31-32

¹ In the beginning was the Word, and the Word was with God, and the Word was God. ² He was with God in the beginning. ³ All things were created through Him, and apart from Him not one thing was created that has been created. ⁴ Life was in Him, and that life was the light of men. ⁵ That light shines in the darkness, yet the darkness did not overcome it. – John 1:1-5

¹⁹ This, then, is the judgment: The light has come into the world, and people loved darkness rather than the light because their deeds were evil. ²⁰ For everyone who practices wicked things hates the light and avoids it, so that his

deeds may not be exposed. ²¹ But anyone who lives by the truth comes to the light, so that his works may be shown to be accomplished by God. – John 3:19-21

¹⁸ Then Jesus came near and said to them, "All authority has been given to Me in heaven and on earth. ¹⁹ Go, therefore, and make disciples of all nations, baptizing them in the name of the Father and of the Son and of the Holy Spirit, ²⁰ teaching them to observe everything I have commanded you. And remember, I am with you always, to the end of the age." – Matthew 28:18-20

¹⁰ When the LORD your God brings you into the land He swore to your fathers Abraham, Isaac, and Jacob that He would give you—a land with large and beautiful cities that you did not build, ¹¹ houses full of every good thing that you did not fill them with, wells dug that you did not dig, and vineyards and olive groves that you did not plant—and when you eat and are satisfied, ¹² be careful not to forget the LORD who brought you out of the land of Egypt, out of the place of slavery. – Deuteronomy 6:10-12

¹ Now faith is the reality of what is hoped for, the proof of what is not seen. ² For our ancestors won God's approval by it. ³ By faith we understand that the universe was created by God's command, so that what is seen has been made from things that are not visible. – Hebrews 11:1-3

SMALL-GROUP QUESTIONS

Over the next few pages you'll find discussion questions, material that may be used as additional discussion points, and a journal exercise for group members to complete away from the group.

"The presence of God is perceived ... by faith, not by feeling."

1. How does the author of Hebrews speak of faith? How does faith differ from feeling?

2. What is it about the presence of God that helps you trust your faith?

LIGHT IN THE DARKNESS

Have you ever gone spelunking (aka caving)? A cave is a very interesting place to experience darkness. When you go into a dark room, often your eyes will adjust to the room and you will be able to make out shapes and figures.

When you go into a deep cave, your eyes do not really adjust. You can hold your hand up in front of your face and not see it. This is why you wear a headlamp when you go spelunking.

When one person in your group turns his or her headlamp on, everything will light up in an instant, exposing all the vast intricacies of the cave.

Even in the dense darkness of a cave, light will dissolve darkness in an instant.

"Don't doubt in the dark what you saw in the light!"

3. We can understand why God might choose to allow trials and testing, but what about seasons of darkness and disorientation? Do you think God withdraws His presence? Explain.

4. How do John 1:1-5 and 3:19-21 create an assurance of hope for you?

"A lot of you feel your way into your beliefs rather than believe your way into your feelings."

5. God built us with emotions. So how do we allow ourselves to experience feelings and emotions without letting them dictate our behavior?

6. How does the cross assure us that God is not absent from our lives?

WELL SAID

"He is there, and he is not silent. There is no use having a silent God. We would not know anything about him. He has spoken and told us what he is and that he existed before all else, and so we have the answer to the existence of what is.

"He is not silent. The reason we have the answer is because the infinite-personal God, the full trinitarian God, has not been silent. He has told us who he is. Couch your concept of inspiration and revelation in these terms, and you will see how it cuts down into the warp and woof of modern thinking." [1]

— Francis Schaeffer, 1972

JOURNAL

This journaling opportunity is designed for group members to utilize at another time. They may choose to answer the questions in the space provided or they may prefer to use the space and time to take a deep question or concern to God.

"We want to fill you up with the promises of God … so that when life shakes you or knocks you over, you spill out God's promises; and when life cuts you, you bleed God's Word."

One of the most common dangers a Christian faces is replacing a love of God with a religious routine that becomes void of the very passion it was born out of. Does that describe you right now? In the past?

Take some time to reflect on the past couple of weeks. How are the promises of God impacting your daily life? How do you want them to?

YOU'RE UP

Everything we need came to us in the death and resurrection of Jesus Christ. There is nothing we could ever do to make Him love us more or less. Even in the darkest days God's Word will flood our souls with the light of the cross and His intentions for our lives. This week you are going to write your own prayer to remind yourself of the truths we can claim as Christians. Include reminders of:

- The redemption given to us by God through Jesus;

- The faith we can have in the cross as a source of hope for what each day will hold;

- Any other promises from the gospel that you feel you need to be reminded of.

- Pray this prayer every day this week and consider sharing it with your group next week.

Next week we finish up our study by looking at the power of the presence of God in our lives. To prepare for the lesson, take a few minutes to read Exodus 34:10-12. You may also want to look at Judges 13:2-5; 16:18-20; Galatians 5:22-26; and Acts 1:7-8.

1. Francis A. Schaeffer, *He Is There and He Is Not Silent* (Carol Stream, IL: Tyndale House Publishers, 2001), 16-17.

Power of God

Everyone grows up wanting to be extraordinary. We are fascinated by superheroes because they have an ability or power that sets them apart from everyone else. We love the stories of Cinderella and King Arthur because they were royalty wrapped in everyday clothing. We identify with Harry Potter because deep down we feel that we are destined to be a part of something greater.

As we grow up, careers and mortgages and child rearing often mute our dreams for greatness. The grind of reality makes stability and security the new targets of our life adventure. As we settle into normalcy, the Scriptures seem more like fairy tales from our childhood than they do our experience. We read of God's miraculous, powerful work in Israel or the early church and our skeptical minds have a hard time believing we are a part of that same, great story.

Maybe ordinary is our destiny after all. Maybe.

WARM UP

Try not to spend too much time here, but let everyone answer the warm-up questions. Getting group members involved early helps create the best small-group environment.

What was your dream job when you were a child—if you could have been anything, what would you have been?

What was it about the idea of that job that filled you with passion?

VIDEO SET UP

The information below sets up the video. It can be read aloud to the group, read by group members ahead of time, or group members can read the information silently while the facilitator sets up the video.

Reading the Exodus account leaves one in awe of how powerfully and specifically God intervened to rescue and deliver His people. The plagues, the pillar of fire, the Red Sea, the manna, and the cloud on Mount Horeb all make it clear God's power was at work.

In the New Testament we see that Jesus was so powerful that just a brush of His clothing healed a woman with a chronic disease. With just a word He brought people back from the dead, made the blind see, and helped the lame walk. The early church experienced the power of God when the Holy Spirit descended upon the apostles at Pentecost, causing them to speak the gospel in languages they'd never even heard before. So where is that power today?

In this final session, J.D. teaches on how the power of God can and should be on display in our lives today. We will look at the extraordinary life we all long to live and how the presence of God comes with the power to do the miraculous for the advancement of the mission of God.

Take a moment to read through the Scriptures on pages 82-83 before watching "Power of God" (15:43). Then discuss the two questions designed as follow-up to the video on the Viewer Guide page.

SHOW VIDEO NOW.

VIEWER GUIDE

Included are two questions designed as follow-up to "Power of God." This time is set aside for discussion within the group about what they heard, how it affected them, and possible applications. These questions may be only a beginning. Feel free to begin the conversation by asking what thoughts, insights, or stories had the most impact on group members.

1.   According to J.D., what is wrong with the term "missional church"?

2.   In this video session, J.D. asks two questions for you to consider about yourself:

    •   Does your life make the unbelieving world marvel?

    •   Are you different from the world around you in your lifestyle and your goals?

    If your answer to either of these questions is "no," what steps can you take to move closer to "yes"?

BIBLICAL BACKGROUND

With music there is usually a story behind the song that helps listeners appreciate the heart and soul behind both the music and the lyrics. Scripture is no different. Below you'll find a brief story behind this week's Scripture intended to provide additional understanding and insight.

The Old Testament consists of God training Israel, as a father trains a child, to be the community that demonstrates the power of God to other nations. Sometimes it was through reigning fire on an altar like in 1 Kings 18 with Elijah and the prophets of Baal. Sometimes it was through improbable victories like Moses' escape from Pharaoh's army through the Red Sea or David's slaying of Goliath. Regardless, a central theme of the Old Testament is that God's presence among His people included the power to make His greatness known to the surrounding nations.

God gives that same power to His church. The power of God is available to the people of God because they live with the presence of God while carrying out the mission of God. God's primary conduit for His power is the church. Acts 1–2 gives us a picture of a powerful God present with His people.

Samson was a man God chose to lead His people with great power. Samson's desire for his own satisfactions, however, outweighed his concern for God's mission. When that became apparent, God's power ceased to be at work in Samson's life.

There is no disconnect between the power of God and the mission of God. The disconnect is between the people of God and the mission of God. Will we step into this rushing power and be used for something great *on His behalf*?

SCRIPTURE

[10] The LORD responded: "Look, I am making a covenant. I will perform wonders in the presence of all your people that have never been done in all the earth or in any nation. All the people you live among will see the LORD work, for what I am doing with you is awe-inspiring. [11] Observe what I command you today. I am going to drive out before you the Amorites, Canaanites, Hittites, Perizzites, Hivites, and Jebusites. [12] Be careful not to make a treaty with the inhabitants of the land that you are going to enter; otherwise, they will become a snare among you.
– Exodus 34:10-12

[2] There was a certain man from Zorah, from the family of Dan, whose name was Manoah; his wife was unable to conceive and had no children. [3] The Angel of the LORD appeared to the woman and said to her, "It is true that you are unable to conceive and have no children, but you will conceive and give birth to a son. [4] Now please be careful not to drink wine or beer, or to eat anything unclean; [5] for indeed, you will conceive and give birth to a son. You must never cut his hair, because the boy will be a Nazirite to God from birth, and he will begin to save Israel from the power of the Philistines." – Judges 13:2-5

[18] When Delilah realized that he had told her the whole truth, she sent this message to the Philistine leaders: "Come one more time, for he has told me the whole truth." The Philistine leaders came to her and brought the money with them. [19] Then she let him fall asleep on her lap and called a man to shave off the seven braids on his head. In this way, she made him helpless, and his strength left him. [20] Then she cried, "Samson, the Philistines are here!" When he awoke from his sleep, he said, "I will escape as I did before and shake myself free." But he did not know that the LORD had left him. – Judges 16:18-20

[22] The fruit of the Spirit is love, joy, peace, patience, kindness, goodness, faith, [23] gentleness, self-control. Against such things there is no law. [24] Now those who belong to Christ Jesus have crucified the flesh with its passions and desires. [25] Since we live by the Spirit, we must also follow the Spirit. [26] We must not become conceited, provoking one another, envying one another. – Galatians 5:22-26

[7] He said to them, "It is not for you to know times or periods that the Father has set by His own authority. [8] But you will receive power when the Holy Spirit has come on you, and you will be My witnesses in Jerusalem, in all Judea and Samaria, and to the ends of the earth." – Acts 1:7-8

SMALL-GROUP QUESTIONS

Over the next few pages you'll find discussion questions, material that may be used as additional discussion points, and a journal exercise for group members to complete away from the group.

> "God doesn't have a mission for His church in the world;
> He's got a church for His mission in the world."

1. Reread Exodus 34:10-12. Why is God going to perform such powerful works in Israel? What will keep the Israelites from experiencing this power?

2. What are the main "snares" in your life?

SOMETHING TO BUILD ON

In 1976 Millard and Linda Fuller founded Habitat for Humanity International (HFHI). The Fullers left careers in the business sector to pursue a life of Christian ministry. The idea for Habitat was born out of a desire to partner with the poor to create affordable housing for all who need it.

It was the belief of the Fullers that all people are created in the image of God and are due a certain level of respect. They sought to merge their entrepreneurial skills with their God-given passion to take the love of Christ to the poor. As a result, HFHI was born.

Perhaps their best-known advocate is former president Jimmy Carter along with his wife Rosalynn. Through their support and countless others God has brought, HFHI has built more than 400,000 houses, sheltering more than 2 million people worldwide. [1]

The Fullers were not superheroes. They were a couple with a desire to honor God and spread the grace they experienced in Christ using the talents and gifts He had given them.

How has God wired you to demonstrate His love for the world?

"Many of you are anointed by God. … God has given you favor and power and blessing and opportunity and … you've used it all for yourself."

3. Samson's story is an example of how God uses even self-centered, sinful people to accomplish His mission. But does that let us off the hook for our bad behavior? Explain.

4. God had a dream for Samson. Samson had the power of God at his disposal but it went unused. What might he have missed by not taking advantage of his greatest strength? What might you be missing by doing the same?

IN THE WORLD BUT NOT OF IT

In A.D. 125 a philosopher named Aristides wrote a letter to the Emperor of Rome evaluating Jews, Greeks, Barbarians, and Christians against one another. This is what he said about the Christians:

> But the Christians, O King, while they went about and made search, have found the truth; ... For they know and trust in God, the Creator of heaven and of earth, in whom and from whom are all things, to whom there is no other god as companion, from whom they received commandments which they engraved upon their minds and observe in hope and expectation of the world which is to come. ... And if there is among them any that is poor and needy, and if they have no spare food, they fast two or three days in order to supply to the needy their lack of food. They observe the precepts of their Messiah with much care, living justly and soberly as the Lord their God commanded them. Every morning and every hour they give thanks and praise to God for His loving-kindnesses toward them; and for their food and their drink they offer thanksgiving to Him. ... And to me there is no doubt but that the earth abides through the supplication of the Christians. But the rest of the nations err and cause error in wallowing before the elements of the world. [2]

"Do people marvel at the fruit of the Spirit in your life?"

5. Read Galatians 5:22-26. How does the fruit of the Holy Spirit lived out in our lives actually display God's power to those around us?

6. There is a danger that we can begin to view the fruit of the Spirit as some sort of checklist we follow to ensure God is happy with us. How do we avoid slipping into such legalism as we evaluate ourselves in light of Galatians 5:22-26?

7. As you wrap up your study of *Presence*, what would you consider a key takeaway for you? Explain.

JOURNAL

This journaling opportunity is designed for group members to utilize at another time. They may choose to answer the questions in the space provided or they may prefer to use the space and time to take a deep question or concern to God.

"Are you different from the world around you in your lifestyle and your goals?"

Consider your life and what you are building toward. What, specifically, is it about your goals and how you live your life that sets you apart from the world? Are there things you can do to set yourself apart more?

YOU'RE UP

This week we've targeted the power of God and how the fruit of the Spirit at work in our lives is where the power of God is visible to the watching world. Consider the following challenges this next week:

- Start praying now about a relationship or interaction you will be involved in this week. Ask God to grant you the fruit of the Spirit. Commit to pray daily for patience and self-control.

- Think of the pockets of people in your community to whom your group can show love and kindness. Who do you think your group could begin serving?

Paul's prayer in Ephesians 3 sums up our hope for you as you complete this study:

14 For this reason I kneel before the Father 15 from whom every family in heaven and on earth is named. 16 I pray that He may grant you, according to the riches of His glory, to be strengthened with power in the inner man through His Spirit, 17 and that the Messiah may dwell in your hearts through faith. I pray that you, being rooted and firmly established in love, 18 may be able to comprehend with all the saints what is the length and width, height and depth of God's love, 19 and to know the Messiah's love that surpasses knowledge, so you may be filled with all the fullness of God. 20 Now to Him who is able to do above and beyond all that we ask or think according to the power that works in us— 21 to Him be glory in the church and in Christ Jesus to all generations, forever and ever. – Ephesians 3:14-21

1. "The History of Habitat," *Habitat for Humanity* [online] 2011, [cited 24 May 2011]. Available on the Internet: *www.habitat.org*.
2. "The Apology of Aristides the Philosopher," *Early Christian Writings* [online], [cited 24 May 2011]. Available on the Internet: *www.earlychristianwritings.com*.

Other titles in the Platform Series

This collection of small group Bible studies features compelling video sermons, straight from the platforms of some of today's most influential pastors. Among the latest is *Have the Funeral* by James MacDonald, which explores the process of forgiveness—from the biblical definition all the way to the official burial of our unforgiveness and life thereafter.

Each study in the series offers six video presentations, one for each session, and a study guide. Visit us online to get more information and free samples.

lifeway.com/platform | 800.458.2772 | LifeWay Christian Stores

LifeWay | Small Group